PINNER

HATCH END, NORTH HARROW AND RAYNERS LANE

A Pictorial History

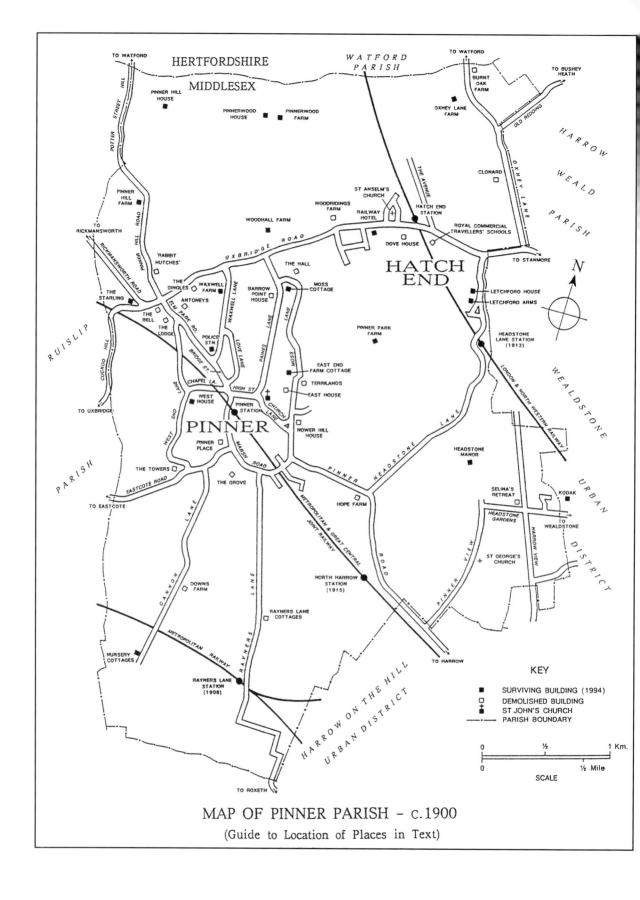

MAP OF PINNER PARISH – c.1900
(Guide to Location of Places in Text)

PINNER

HATCH END, NORTH HARROW
AND RAYNERS LANE
A Pictorial History

Patricia A. Clarke
and the Pinner Local History Society

Phillimore

1994

Published by
PHILLIMORE & CO. LTD.,
Shopwyke Manor Barn, Chichester, West Sussex

ISBN 0 85033 898 0

Printed and bound in Great Britain by
BIDDLES LTD.
Guildford, Surrey

List of Illustrations

Frontispiece: Map of Pinner Parish

Acknowledgments

These must include acknowledgments to people and sources. All the members of Pinner Local History Society's research group have helped in some way in the making and checking of this book, in particular Bernard Harrison, Ken Kirkman, Iris Long, Graham Elcombe and Jim Golland. The help of Bob Thomson, from the Local History Library and Collection of the London Borough of Harrow, has been essential and unstinting.

As to the sources, the research, both published and unpublished, of members of the Pinner History Society has been pillaged, as also has that of Pinner's most influential local historian, the late Edwin Ware. His work, and the photographs that he took or collected, whether published or unpublished, have inspired all who came after him.

The map of Pinner was drawn by Tony Venis.

Errors are sure to have survived—they always do—and we would be pleased to have your correction of them so that we may correct ourselves or the record, as appropriate.

Illustration Acknowledgments

The author wishes to thank the following for the use of illustrations; Aerofilms Ltd, 166; David Bednall, 155; Greater London Record Office (Photographic Library), 47, 58, 84, 91, 119, 124; Patricia Clarke, 9, 36, 37, 42-3, 48, 71, 109, 111, 122, 149; Francis Critchley, 102-3; Cyril Ellement, 35, 85-6; Norman Ellement, 158, 170; Ivy Field, 81, 162-5; Charles Peters, 16; Alison Greenwood, 11, 8, 181; David Gurney, 153-4; *Harrow Observer*, 29, 131; Ken Kirkman, 136; J. Laidlaw, 120; London Underground, 53, 57; Iris Long, 49, 54, 147, 151, 152, 159-60; National Portrait Gallery, 135; Pinner Association, 74-5, 110; Jette Parsey, 1; Betty Price, 140; Marian Russell, 113; Peter Saunders, 173; Hilda Sharpe, 94; Phyllis Tee, 30, 41; Paul Thompson, 115; Richard Trusselle, 17, 20-1; United Free Church, Pinner, 95; Susanna Vedel, 62; Sylvia Venis, 134, 137; Martin Verden, 65-6. Pinner Local History Society's illustrations, 7, 15, 23, 26-8, 32-4, 39, 44, 51-2, 55, 69-70, 76, 78, 80, 82-3, 87, 90, 97-9, 105, 107, 117, 121, 126, 128-30, 140, 148, 169, 177-8, include many given by the following—Mrs. Barron, Mrs. Bentley, Mrs. Ostafew, Bert Parslow, Jack Rackliff, Mrs. Sargeant, Miss Squires, Mrs. Tennant and Mrs. Warburg. For the remaining large number of illustrations we are indebted to the London Borough of Harrow Local History Collection at the Civic Centre Library; among them are many from the Pinner in the Vale collection of the late Edwin Ware.

Introduction

The beginnings

People ask 'How old is Pinner?' and the reply must be 'No one knows'. As it is today part of the London Borough of Harrow in the north western part of Greater London, so in times past it was part of the manor and parish of Harrow in Middlesex. A manor was a medieval estate owned by a lord. Harrow was a very large manor containing several separate villages in medieval times—Alperton, Wembley, Preston, Uxendon, Kenton, Harrow Weald, Pinner, Roxeth, Greenhill and, on the hill itself, Sudbury. None is mentioned in Domesday Book, however, because the purpose of the compilers was to record major land holdings, rather than smaller places, and so it is only Harrow, the manor itself, which is recorded.

Domesday Book shows that the Archbishop of Canterbury held Harrow, keeping some 30 per cent of the land for his own use, and that the population consisted of a priest, three knights who had seven tenants, 104 villagers and two slaves (or landless people). All of these, except the priest, were probably heads of families and may therefore represent a population of about 500 in the manor of Harrow.

There is nothing to show which villages these people lived in, nor how many villages there were at that date. Wembley and Roxeth were definitely in existence, for they were mentioned in documents dated 824 and 845 respectively, but there are no written records to confirm the existence of the other villages.

The earliest known occurrence of the name Pinner dates from 1231, when it formed part of the name of Godfrey of Pinner. Three years later a chapel in Pinner was referred to in a document concerning Harrow church, evidence that there must have been a population large enough to warrant one.

Medieval Pinner

The resources of the manor were shared between the villagers though ownership lay with the lord. The normal country village was self-supporting, so each villager had to cultivate his share of the common agricultural land. In Pinner most of this land was contained in three fields, which lay between the line made today by Pinner Road, Marsh Road and West End Lane in the north, and the one made by Lucas Avenue and Drake Avenue in the south. These fields were separated from each other by Rayners Lane, with Longfield to the east, Middlefield to the west, and Cannon Lane between Middlefield and the westernmost one, Downfield. The largest common pasture, for the use of the animals, lay around the present Pinner Green, and stretched northward to Potter Street, at which point it changed into woodland. By the 14th century, there were several hamlets apart from the High Street, all of which are still identifiable—West End, Nower Hill, East End, Bury Pond (Barrow Point) and Hatch End.

In return for the use of the land, the villagers spent part of their time cultivating the lord's 30 per cent. The archbishop had four large estates in Harrow and three of them were in Pinner. The most distinctive was Pinner Park, a deer reserve, comprising some 250 acres enclosed by a bank and fence, which retained the lord's deer safely within it rather than serving as a hunting park. It was referred to as early as 1274 and survives today as Halls

Farm. The present farmhouse replaces an earlier moated house. Some of the land has been lost to the railway, and some given over to sports grounds, otherwise the area and boundary has changed little. Most of the bank has been despoiled over the last century or so, but some stretches remain near Little Moss Lane and Woodridings Avenue.

The second estate, lying north of Uxbridge Road, bounded on the east by Woodridings Close and on the west reaching almost to Pinner Hill Road, was the sub-manor of Woodhall—a large farm of about 300 acres, with a farmhouse on the site of the present Woodhall Farm in Woodhall Drive. The earliest reference to it is dated 1234.

The third of the estates was Headstone Manor, acquired by the archbishop from one of his tenants in 1344. Like Woodhall it was a large farm, about 200 acres in extent, but was different from Woodhall in that here the archbishop built himself a new house, Headstone Manor House, in which to reside when he was in the area. His normal business was in London or Canterbury, so that Harrow's lord of the manor was an occasional visitor only. Part of the house still stands.

John Stratford, the archbishop who developed Headstone Manor, also secured the royal charter for Pinner's famous fair. On 30 May 1336 two fairs each year were authorised, one on the anniversary of the birth of St John the Baptist and the other on the anniversary of his beheading. The first has taken place annually ever since then, even during wartime, and always in the streets of the village, though the date has moved from St John's Day, 24 June, to the Wednesday after the Spring Bank Holiday. Of the second fair nothing more has ever been heard, nor of the weekly market which was authorised in the same charter.

St John the Baptist's Church

In 1321 the rebuilding of St John's Church was finished, and it was re-consecrated with proper ceremony by a visiting bishop. Just as Pinner was part of the manor of Harrow, so it was part of the parish of Harrow. St Mary's was the parish church; St John's was merely a chapel of ease, a special facility which meant that Pinner's residents did not have to travel to Harrow each Sunday. Clergy were provided and paid for by the rector of Harrow, who received all the offerings and tithes of Pinner. Pinner did not become a parish in its own right until 1766.

The general rebuilding means that most of St John's Church—the chancel, nave and aisles—are of one architectural period, an unusual feature for a village church. The transepts, with windows of early English style, may be older than the rest of the church. The tower and porch were added during the 15th century, and most of the windows were replaced then or in the 16th century; those in the transepts and at the west end of the two aisles are exceptions. The font is 15th century. Monuments earlier than the 18th century are few. The oldest is a chrisom brass commemorating Anne Bedingfeld who died on 23 February 1580 at the age of about one month and is depicted in her swaddling clothes. The most beautiful monument is the black and white marble wall tablet to the memory of Christopher Clitherow of Pinner Hill, who died in 1685 aged 32. The chancel aisle, in which it is now to be found, was built in 1859 to increase the capacity, and was converted to a Lady Chapel in 1938. There is a spectacular tombstone in the churchyard, like a giant wedge or pyramid about 20 feet high with what looks like a coffin protruding from its sides. It was raised by John Claudius Loudon to the memory of his father, William, who died in 1809, with whom he had farmed at Woodhall Farm, experimenting with new methods. It is quite a curiosity and several fanciful tales have been told about a body in the suspended coffin.

Chalk workings

The church is built of flint, much or all of which must have come from local chalk workings. Such workings were of considerable value, not just for the flint but also for the chalk, which was used both to improve the heavy clay soil and as a component of plaster for house building. In medieval times the major local source was at the northern end of Waxwell Lane behind Waxwell Farm, the grounds of which now cover much of the uneven surface of the quarry. The Dell was laid out in the deepest part in 1964. By the end of the Tudor period these diggings were exhausted and quarrying moved north of Uxbridge Road. By the 19th century shafts were being sunk further up the hill towards Pinner Wood in order to extract the chalk.

16th century

In 1545 the Archbishop of Canterbury ceased to be lord of the manor of Harrow. Henry VIII, having run through most of the spoils of the monasteries he had dissolved, cast about for other things to turn to account. He saw Harrow, and obliged the archbishop of the day— Thomas Cranmer, who had granted the king his divorce from Katherine of Aragon and helped him to set up the Church of England—to give him the manor in exchange for lands elsewhere. Within a matter of weeks the king had sold it to Sir (later Lord) Edward North.

To the people of Pinner this change probably made little difference—their lives would have continued in the usual agricultural round. But Sir Edward, like many other men who bought up church property, made a survey of his new estate, and in it we can read the names of the tenant farmers of Pinner, work out where they lived and see the rents they paid. The most prosperous local families included the Edlins, who occupied several farms, including the present Oxhey Lane Farm and Elmdene, in Church Lane; the Readings, from amongst whom the bailiff of Headstone Manor was usually chosen, and who occupied farms which included the present Sweetmans Hall in West End Lane and Tudor Cottage in Moss Lane; the Streets, one of whom usually ran Woodhall manor for the archbishop, but whose other properties can no longer be seen; and the Birds, deputy-keepers of Pinner Park, and occupiers, among other places, of Church Farm at the top of the High Street. These were the men of influence in Pinner, the ones whose word would have counted when local matters like the repair of the church, the relief of the poor, or the mending of the roads were under discussion. These influential families also built the timber-framed houses for which Pinner is notable. The largest collection is in the High Street, but nearly every one of the old medieval hamlets can still boast one. Many of them do not show their true character, for succeeding owners have covered them in brick. In High Street, Church Farm, no.27 and no.9 are well disguised as are The Bay House and Elmdene, along Church Lane.

17th and 18th centuries

There were no aristocrats in Pinner at this time, but Londoners with money were taking an interest in the place. Among them was Christopher Clitherow who, as Lord Mayor of London, was knighted in 1635. He spent part of the fortune he had amassed in business, as a member (and then Master) of the Ironmongers' Company and the East India Company, in acquiring several acres of Pinner Hill on which he built a house. He was succeeded by a son and a grandson, each named Christopher, the latter being the one commemorated by the marble tablet in Pinner Church.

During this period Lord North's descendants were selling off parts of the manor, especially the large estates such as Headstone Manor, Pinner Park and Woodhall Manor, which attracted more buyers from outside. In 1630 William Pennifather, Sheriff of London, bought

Woodhall Manor; Thomas Hutchinson of London purchased Pinner Park, which had been converted from deer park to farm during the 16th century; and Simon Rewse bought Headstone Manor, of which he was already the tenant. The Rewse family provides Pinner's most interesting piece of civil war history. Simon's second son, Francis, fought on the side of King Charles I, and in doing so earned himself a knighthood from the king, but trouble for his family from the Parliamentarians, in the shape of a £300 fine which was secured (rather like a mortgage) on his share of Headstone. When, or even if, it was settled is not known, but it was causing trouble to a later purchaser in 1653.

Pinner continued to be primarily a place of farmers and agricultural labourers, with a sprinkling of gentlemen plus a few local traders supplying necessities such as bread, meat, groceries and ale. Most of the identifiable old medieval holdings continued as farms. Several of the former farmhouses still stand—Waxwell Farm, Sweetmans Hall, Pinnerwood House, Bee Cottage, Elmdene, East End Farm Cottage, Moss Cottage, Letchford House. Some, like Oxhey Lane Farm, West House, West End Farm, have been rebuilt. Others have vanished—Park Gate, Dove House, Antoneys, Nower Hill, Dears Farm, East House and Weatherleys.

The gentlemen who came to Pinner sometimes built themselves new houses, but more often improved the original dwellings by rebuilding or extension. The best surviving examples of new ones are Pinner House (early 18th century) in Church Lane, no.20 Waxwell Lane and no.32 High Street (mid-18th century), and 58 High Street and The Lawn in Elm Park Road (early 19th century). One or two minor aristocrats were resident in Pinner. The Marquis of Caernarvon bought Pinner Hill House for his cousin, Lady Jane Brydges, in 1755, and it was rebuilt towards the end of the century, perhaps by her. The Hall, which stood at the corner of Uxbridge Road and Paines Lane, was the residence for a decade or two before 1788 of Martha, widow of Lord Henry Beauclerc who was of the family of the Dukes of St Albans.

Population

It has been estimated that at the beginning of the 18th century about 660 people lived in Pinner, but the number had fallen to some 530 by mid-century, probably as part of a trend common to much of England, but also because of a recent epidemic. The census returns show that the figure was 761 in 1801, and during the 19th century the population rose considerably, following the common trend once again. In 1851 the number stood at 1,310, and by 1901 it was 3,366. Immigration from elsewhere augmented the natural increase, coming especially from the counties to the west and north, Buckinghamshire, Berkshire, Bedfordshire and Oxfordshire. By 1951 the figure for the area roughly equivalent to 19th-century Pinner was about 45,000.

The early 19th century

Early in the 19th century the process of enclosure was applied to the manor of Harrow, entailing the abolition of the shared ownership of the common fields with the accompanying need for harmonisation in work practice and crops sown. The land was reallocated on the basis of existing land ownership and common rights, each new owner having unfettered individual rights within his own boundaries. The Act empowering the enclosure was passed by Parliament in 1803 and the process of enquiry and allocation was completed in 1817. Some people ended up with perhaps only an acre as their share of the old common fields, while others had several hundred. There was much selling and exchange of holdings, large and small, and a few new farms were formed during the following couple of decades—Burnt Oak at the north-east end of Oxhey Lane, Mill Farm and Pinner Hill Farm along Pinner Hill

Road, Temple Farm at the junction of West End Lane and Eastcote Road, and Downs Farm half way along Cannon Lane. Farms which increased in size included that of Daniel Hill of Church Farm, who did not build himself a new farmhouse where most of his land now lay along Rayners Lane, but built cottages for his workers there instead and kept Church Farm as his farmhouse.

The London to Birmingham Railway was built in 1837 and passed through the north-east part of Pinner, cutting through some of the farms—Pinner Park Farm, Hatch End Farm (now Letchford House), Dove House Farm, Woodhall Farm and Oxhey Lane Farm, and causing problems of internal access. A station named Pinner was opened in 1842, renamed Pinner and Hatch End in 1897, Hatch End for Pinner in 1920, and at last simply Hatch End in 1948. It began with a basic service of five trains a day, with return fares to London costing 3s. 6d. (17.5p) for first class, 2s. 6d. (12.5p) for second, and 1s. 6d. (7.5p) for third-class tickets. There were no nearby customers other than farmers at the places above mentioned, but here, as elsewhere in the London area, the railway company decided to encourage the building of houses in the vicinity and in 1853 offered free first-class season tickets for a number of years to persons occupying houses near the station in Pinner worth not less than £50 annual rent. The move succeeded— in 1855 there was a new estate near the station, known as Woodridings, whose attractions included a free first-class season ticket valid for 13 years for each house. The number of years was governed by the distance from Euston— similar offers at Harrow were for 12 years, at Watford for 14 years.

The residents of the Woodridings estate were Pinner's first commuters, having well paid and regular positions in law, commerce, trade, publishing, the civil service and the church, or else living on private means such as annuities. The style of the houses resembled those being built in the environs of London at Chalk Farm, Notting Hill Gate and Hammersmith, though those in Pinner were smaller and built in pairs.

Before the middle of the 19th century the increasing numbers of artisans and labourers were accommodated in subdivided property or in new small cottages, mostly made of wood, erected at Pinner Green or along Marsh Road. Not one of them remains. From about 1840 new cottages were usually built in brick, in pairs or terraces, often financed from savings by local traders or even labourers, and intended as an investment against old age or misfortune.

The later 19th century

There were still many miles of countryside between the indubitably rural Pinner and London. Although the railway station had little perceptible effect on the village the basis of its economy was nevertheless changing. In 1851 about 42 per cent of its population was engaged in agricultural or related occupations. By 1881 that proportion had declined to about 15 per cent and had been replaced as leader by domestic service, which had risen from about 25 to about 30 per cent. London's voracious demand for hay to feed the horse-power necessary to its existence, and for dairy products for its residents, promoted the less labour intensive, non-arable types of farming. At the same time the gradual increase in the numbers of middle-class people living in Pinner, including the commuters at Woodridings, kept the demand for domestic servants more than buoyant and enlarged the scope of employment in such areas as shopkeeping, transport and carriage, and construction.

Pinner should not be thought of as a backwater, even though it was rural and rail travel was not yet cheap enough to turn most of its inhabitants into commuters. There was plenty of communication with neighbouring places. From 1855 there was a weekly newspaper, the

Harrow Gazette containing national as well as local news. There was a post office in one shop or another in the High Street from 1823 until it moved into exclusive premises, including a telephone switchboard, at 23 High Street (now Bishops Walk) in 1903. National movements had their reflections in Pinner, such as the branch of the Manchester Unity of Oddfellows, established as the Loyal British Queen Lodge of Pinner in 1845, and later based at 31 Waxwell Lane. The temperance movement came to Pinner in the shape of the *Cocoa Tree* tavern at the top of the High Street (no.64), specially built in 1878 by William Barber, a judge who lived at Barrow Point House, in order to provide an alternative to the other dozen places which sold alcohol.

In particular there was the influence of the local school, part of the educational system spreading throughout the country. Dame schools existed from time to time, and so did academies, schools taking fee-paying day and boarding pupils, not necessarily local children, although there is little information about them. There are intermittent references early in the 19th century to a church school and a Sunday school which the majority of Pinner's boys and girls could attend if their parents wished, probably for a small charge. In 1841 a village school for about a hundred children was built in brick where the gardens are now, at the bottom of the High Street, under the auspices of the National Society. Within 25 years it was too small and a replacement was built along Marsh Road, reached by a short new lane. Any child could attend on payment of a few pence, and most seem to have done so. The teachers, usually a husband and wife combination, were assisted by monitors and, like children in other places, Pinner boys and girls began to find themselves able to compete for clerical and teaching work, incidentally increasing their own mobility. This school was demolished in 1980, but School Lane is still there.

The Commercial Travellers' School was entirely separate. It was a residential school for the orphans of commercial travellers, which transferred to Hatch End from Wanstead in 1855. The Prince Consort performed the opening ceremony, coming by the most modern form of transport to the new station from Euston. During the 20th century a grammar school education was provided, but a want of pupils obliged it to close in 1967.

There was plenty of local recreational activity in late 19th-century Pinner, and many entertainments were staged in the former school building at the foot of the High Street (turned into use as a parish hall) and in the rooms of the *Cocoa Tree*. There were concerts, with musical items both vocal and instrumental, recitations, readings, talks, magic lantern shows, and sometimes plays. The participants were local and ranged from the more genteel members of society playing piano or violin, to more workaday ones declaiming a favourite narrative poem. The Pinner Silver Band performed frequently. Village sports days were held occasionally. Sometimes there would be a parade or drill by the local rifle corps or the Pinner Fire Brigade. Flower shows by the Pinner Horticultural Society were popular and usually had the added attraction of being held in the grounds of a large local mansion such as The Hall, or Barrow Point House. The two royal jubilees were celebrated by the whole village with a combination of home-made events.

Increasing pressure of population led to the creation of the new parish of St Anselm's at Hatch End in 1895, incorporating the temporary chapel of ease called All Saints', which had been established in Devonshire Road in 1865 to serve the Woodridings estate. Non-conformists had meanwhile established their own places of worship. The Methodists built a chapel in Chapel Lane in 1844, after having worshipped for several years in domestic premises nearby. The Baptists built their chapel a few yards to the east in 1859, and it was after these two premises that the lane was named. The Baptist chapel, displaced by the

Metropolitan Railway, was rebuilt in Marsh Road in 1885, but the Methodists did not need to move to their present site in Love Lane till 1918. The first Roman Catholic church, St Luke's, was also built in Love Lane in 1915.

A new station and its consequences

The Metropolitan Railway station in Pinner was opened on Whit Monday 1885, just a couple of days in advance of Pinner Fair. The demolition of several properties—houses and cottages in Marsh Road, the former workhouse near the *George*, cottages and the chapel in Chapel Lane—plus the construction of the two overhead bridges, must have made a strong impression on the villagers. The London and North Western Railway (successor of the London and Birmingham Railway) responded to its new competitor by inaugurating a horse-drawn bus service from the centre of Pinner to its station on the main line. The steady penetration of this part of Middlesex by railway lines drew the attention of those living in London to the area, and speculative building began to appear near the centre. In the decades either side of 1900 development was patchy. The houses were intended mostly for the middle-class market. In 1893 the *Harrow Gazette* observed that the locally born working class were having difficulty finding cottages to live in; only a few in The Chase and a couple of short terraces in Rickmansworth Road seem to have been intended for them.

There were small stretches of better roadside development, in the form of single or paired houses at the junction of Pinner Road with Nower Hill, and along Marsh Road, Eastcote Road and Elm Park Road, usually taken up by clerks, professional men, academics and London traders. New roads were laid out. The larger part of the extensive Barrow Point House estate was utilised for development and Barrowpoint Avenue, Oakhill Avenue, Leighton and Avenue Roads were set out on it and gradually filled over the next twenty or so years. The new houses were well built, with plenty of the red brick, tile hanging, white woodwork, plastering, bay windows and porches typical of the time. In the older roads the houses tended to be more spacious still, set in larger gardens, more varied in design—Paines Lane, Moss Lane, the northern part of Waxwell Lane, and the eastern side of Elm Park Road have typical examples. Many had a small room for a resident servant.

Rather more modest accommodation was provided in Melrose and Kingsley Roads off Pinner Road, which were lined with red-brick terraces and provided with a corner shop.

The Metropolitan Railway Surplus Lands Company built one of its earliest estates on surplus lands either side of the railway line between Church Lane and Marsh Road. Only the southern half was tackled at first, with modest terraces along Marsh Road and a new thoroughfare, Cecil Park, whose earliest houses were very large and high, reminiscent of some at Bedford Park in Chiswick. The northern half, with Grange Gardens, was developed between the wars.

A handful of purpose-built shops erected in Bridge Street between 1865 and 1880 had shown that the rising demand for retail outlets was already beginning to exceed the capacity of the High Street. The trend was confirmed when a new parade of shops, faced with fashionable timber framing, arose at the corner of Love Lane and Bridge Street after the Howard Place site was put up for development in 1908.

By 1914 new neighbourhoods were appearing away from the centre of Pinner. Towards Hatch End the Dove House estate was turning into a residential area. On the eastern boundary many new streets overlapped the dividing line between Harrow and Pinner; in 1911 a church was built in Pinner View for the new parish of St George, and North Harrow station on the Metropolitan Line was opened in 1915. Rayners Lane station on the Uxbridge branch of the Metropolitan Railway was established in 1904, but by contrast remained a small, solitary halt among the fields for another two decades.

First World War to the Second World War

More than 400 men from Pinner served in some capacity during the First World War, and those who died are remembered on the War Memorial unveiled at the top of High Street in 1921. The chief home front recollections were of the hospital for wounded servicemen in Pinner Place, and a view of the episode in which Captain Leefe Robinson, V.C., shot down a Zeppelin over Cuffley in 1916.

Between the two world wars the physical expansion of London reached Pinner and went beyond it. The fields disappeared, the lanes were lined with dwellings, new roads were built and large new estates laid out. No longer were the old shopping centres, the church, the school, the bus, sufficient to cater for local needs, but had to be duplicated in new centres. Near the old centre and to the north of the former parish, developments remained individual and often very select. They lay within the swathe of Middlesex in which the Metropolitan Railway was fostering development with great assiduity, giving it the name Metroland, wherein the houses were old world but full of every modern convenience, set in verdant lanes yet close to station, schools and shops, which looked out upon country scenes while being within 20 to 30 minutes of the heart of the world's greatest city.

Further south Pinner was covered with less ambitious housing—detached, and especially semi-detached, houses and bungalows. As a consequence of government policy to promote the provision of houses by local authorities, groups of council houses appeared along Pinner Road near North Harrow and at the foot of Pinner Hill Road. The new buildings seldom exceeded a height of two storeys. Blocks of flats were rare, and privately owned; they were usually designated a court. Those at Rayners Lane were fairly plain, but Capel Gardens and Pinner Court in Pinner Road, and Elm Park Court at Pinner Green, were full of stylish 1930 characteristics, such as angular framing to doors, windows and private balconies, smooth white stucco walls, and green roofs of Mediterranean-style pantiles.

People poured in. Times were changing and most of the newcomers were the owners of their homes, burdened with mortgages, it is true, but enjoying gardens and the new style of suburban life as never before. The concomitant of expansion was the fragmentation of the former cohesive nature of Pinner society, impossible to maintain because of the vast numbers, but replaced to some degree by smaller communities.

There was no shortage of things to do locally. Cinema and radio offered entertainment for languid moments, but the more active pursuits—sports on tennis courts, playing fields and golf courses, amateur dramatics, Scouts and Guides, cycling and hiking—were well provided for in the new communities. Each had its shopping centre with representatives of chain shops like Woolworth, Boots, United or Express Dairies, and sometimes a cinema—the Langham in Pinner itself, the Embassy at North Harrow, and the Grosvenor (later the Odeon) at Rayners Lane. More new Church of England parishes were created—St Alban's at North Harrow and St Edmund's in Rickmansworth Road—and were interspersed with other denominations, such as the Methodists and St John Fisher's Roman Catholic church at North Harrow, the Baptists and Quakers at Rayners Lane, and, in the early years of the Second World War, a synagogue in what had once been the Baptist Chapel in Marsh Road. Under the Education Act five primary schools were provided—Pinner Park, Cannon Lane, Longfield, Roxbourne and Pinner Wood, a secondary school called Headstone (now Nower Hill), and Pinner Grammar School in Beaulieu Drive. Private educational establishments, from kindergarten to grammar school, flourished.

Pinner remained overwhelmingly residential, with a very strong middle-class flavour. Industry and commerce made no significant impact.

The Second World War affected Pinner much as it did other London suburbs. Most of the younger men were conscripted into the armed forces, while at home bombs sometimes fell, and air raid shelters were hastily built in streets and gardens. The Home Guard and Air Raid Precautions units, and many other Civil Defence activities, took up a good deal of time, and so did the raising of funds for the war effort.

After the Second World War

Population continued to rise after the last world war, reaching 46,651 in 1961. The original extent of Pinner faded from memory, not only because the new pre-war focal centres had loosened its identity, but because the increasing possession of the car made individuals less dependent on their neighbours for support and company. There are noticeable differences between various parts of modern Pinner.

Pinner Village

The centre is now very mixed, having the largest concentration of old buildings, churches, shops and offices, as well as a station. Pressure for residential re-development is strong and flats and town houses of several storeys have appeared in the last 20 years along Chapel Lane, Marsh Road, Nower Hill, Elm Park Road, Paines Lane and Waxwell Lane.

Pinner Hill

Pinner Hill and the area north of Uxbridge Road contain extremes. On the top of the hill among the private roads are some of the most expensive, extensive and individual houses in Pinner (though even here infilling takes place); they were begun during the 1920s upon that part of the Pinner Hill House estate not used for the golf course. At the southern end of the hill is one of the council estates of the 1920s, much of it rebuilt as flats.

Hatch End

Hatch End is now centred upon the shopping parades along Uxbridge Road west of Hatch End Station, but originally it was a hamlet in Headstone Lane in the vicinity of Letchford House. Even after the station was opened, by the London to Birmingham Railway, the name of a nearby farm, Woodridings, was used as a sort of address. Not until the words 'Hatch End' were added to the station name and the Dove House estate was developed at the end of the 19th century did the name begin to shift, and since the building of the shops during the 1930s few people recollect that Hatch End was once elsewhere. The old Woodridings estate has been redeveloped out of existence, except for the public house and a pair of houses in Wellington Road. North of Uxbridge Road the Artagen estate built to the west in the 1930s has many of the neat characteristics found in Hampstead Garden Suburb. Further east the layout is very spacious and varied, though new dwellings close to the station exhibit some of the most closely set houses in Pinner. There is a very high incidence of restaurants among the shops, but it is early days to observe the effect of the new supermarket which opened east of the station in 1992.

North Harrow and Headstone

Though Harrow View was laid out in 1854 nothing was built in the Pinner part of it until the 1890s, and that was effectively development outward from Harrow. St George's parish was created to serve what was really a suburb of Harrow. The earliest building at North Harrow, the so-called county roads laid out before and after the First World War, likewise amounted to tentacles from Harrow. Once the station was opened in 1915 the area achieved its own identity, and between the wars it acquired a shopping centre, public house, churches and the Embassy cinema, replaced by a bowling alley and a supermarket after it closed in 1963. Most of the streets contain semi-detached houses, and there are few terraces, even in the council estate.

Rayners Lane

Attention did not turn to south Pinner until the late 1920s. Harrow Garden Village was built north of the railway line, using such devices as the close, the green, the retention of existing mature trees and the variation of house design to create a desirable estate of the Metroland type. Over sixty years Dutch Elm disease, car parking and infilling have somewhat weakened the effect. Because the land south of the railway line had been in one ownership it was very suitable for development on a large scale by T. F. Nash Ltd. With the creation of over twenty streets, the distribution of building materials by means of an internal railway, the benefit of economies of scale, and a layout primarily in short terraces, the houses were among the least expensive in Pinner. The cinema in the shopping centre at Rayners Lane is the only one in Pinner still standing, though it is now a bar. In recent years the centre has suffered from not containing one of the big supermarket chain stores, and yet being surrounded by other centres which do.

Pinner today

This is not the place for a dissertation upon recent social changes and their causes except to note their effect on the local fabric. The car, redevelopment and shopping changes have been the most noticeable features. Office blocks are the most novel part of the Pinner scene, especially along Marsh Road where their incongruous height dissipates the residential appearance, and at Rayners Lane where they are not out of place visually among the shops and rising level of the land. Flats are more numerous, both in the form of large estates, as in the council estate on the site of the house called The Grove, and the private one where Dove House used to be at Hatch End, and as smaller blocks replacing individual houses in several streets, as along Waxwell Lane, the northern ends of West End Lane and Elm Park Road, Devonshire Road, and east of the allotments in Uxbridge Road. The generously sized gardens of Edwardian Pinner are particularly susceptible to backland development, as the new clusters between Elm Park Road and West End Lane, and at Copperfields off Nower Hill, show quite clearly. The appetite of the car for parking space on road, hard standing or car park is in danger of eroding the leafy appearance. Food superstores press the centre of Pinner and deeply affect the pattern of trade; High Street is quieter during the day than it can have been for many decades, but its attractiveness contributes to the popularity of its public houses. No cinemas now function in Pinner, but you could eat out at a different place every day or night for a fortnight. Fast food shops have arrived after a long struggle. Not surprisingly, opinion on the benefit to Pinner of all these changes is divided.

Nevertheless, many people are still in love with Pinner and try to preserve as much as possible of its village character and pleasant look. It has several conservation areas and the Pinner Association is very vigilant. Parts of north Pinner lie within the Green Belt, so an open aspect is maintained along the hilly northern border. Even today there are three farms in Pinner—Halls Farm in Pinner Park produces milk and yogurt, Oxhey Lane Farm near the Hertfordshire boundary, until recently a dairy farm, is now seeking to diversify, and Pinner Wood Farm is a livestock and stud farm. The rural scene survives.

PATRICIA A. CLARKE

1. This is the first known picture of Pinner High Street, a watercolour painted by a member of the Procter family. Most of the buildings in it still stand today. Since it shows West House as rebuilt early in the 19th century, but does not include no.39 High Street which was built in the early 1820s, the date is probably about 1820. The costume of the workman fits that date.

2. Perhaps the earliest photograph of Pinner, *c*.1850. There are still tiny garden plots in front of the *Queen's Head* and Wakefield House (no.32)—there are flowers and even a tree in the latter one. No pavement has yet been made. The sign hanging outside no.26 shows that it too has become a public house, the *White Hart*. The house to the left of the church was called Belle Vue.

3. One of the earliest photographs of Pinner, thought to be about 1862, shows St John's Church before the churchyard fence was replaced by a wall in 1869. There were more memorials in the churchyard then, many of them wooden headboards.

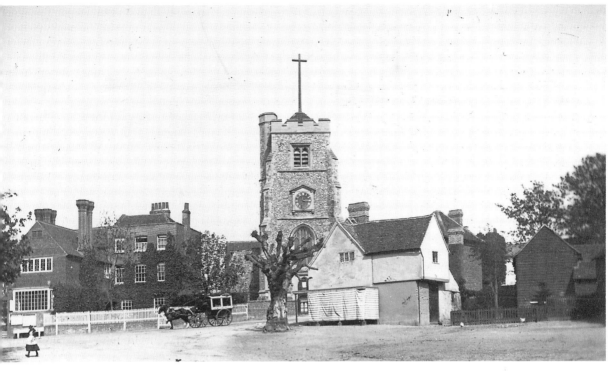

4.   The top of the High Street, *c.*1892. Belle Vue became the *Cocoa Tree* in 1878 when its left-hand part was rebuilt as a temperance tavern at the cost of William Barber of Barrow Point House, to the design of the architect Sir Ernest George. It soon became very popular with day-trippers. Piercy's butcher's shop, protected from the sun by an awning, is a 17th-century house and the building to its right, with the pointed roof, is its old slaughterhouse. In front of the church is the gnarled town tree, which collapsed in 1898. The Pinner bus is about to turn up Paines Lane.

5.   Church Farm, a 16th-century building at the top of the High Street opposite the church, ceased to be a farmhouse in 1906. The picture was taken when the green in front was still private property—it was given to the village in 1922, having been in private ownership since enclosure in 1817. Although the house does not look very different from now, the old farm barns, to the left, were replaced in the 1920s by the house called Farmside.

6.   This range of buildings was demolished about 1933 to make way for Grange Court. In this picture, taken *c*.1920, they are (right to left); Hedges Cottages, Gurney & Ewer, motor engineers (previously the *Hand in Hand*), un-named wooden cottages, probably 17th century, a later building with a range of shops, the barn used by Philip Odell, decorator, and Ashby's timber yard. There is a new town tree.

7.   The lower part of the High Street is prominent in this photograph, dated *c*.1870. Almost every building on the left has been rebuilt or greatly changed since then except for the shop at the extreme left (no.7). The shop next to it, probably Ben Sheepwash's grocery store, was later combined with part of the weather-boarded house to become no.9. James Bedford and his father, both tailors, lived here and successively held the position of parish clerk for a combined total of 69 years. When Edwin Ware, the next parish clerk moved in, parish council meetings were held in the front room. Beyond the fence of no.11, another shop has been rebuilt as nos.13-15, and the next two houses have been rebuilt as nos.17-19. It has been said that the top-hatted man is Thomas Grimwood, a builder (*see* no.43), and the lad is George Ellement, son of Thomas Ellement (*see* no.85). Higher up the street two bullocks also seem interested in the camera.

8.   By 1892-1898 James Petley had taken over from Sheepwash and perhaps it is he who stands in his shopman's apron at the shop-front. The wooden canopy over John Lee's butcher's shop next door is still in place today. The *Crown* had been an inn since the late 17th century, though it did not have this name until the middle of the 18th century. The coach to London left from here at the end of the 18th century. Across the road four new tall houses built by Daniel Gurney proved hard to let at the rent he wanted, so were gradually converted into shops, a process half completed by the time this photograph was taken. The fact that the shutters are closed in daytime means that the shops are not let.

9.   The scene had changed by 1900. The *Crown* was pulled down in 1897 and replaced by the present nos.1-5 (no.5 is on the left). Petley's has been enlarged and rebuilt, and so has Kingham's, the grocer on the other side of the weather-boarded shop, and the houses beyond. Another of Gurney's houses has been converted, but the shutters suggest they are still hard to let. The adjoining cycle business was a result of the cycling craze. The shop on the right was the post and telegraph office run by Robert Rowe, who was also a draper.

10. The changes made at the turn of the century can be seen much better in this photograph of January 1934. Charles Johnson is about to move shop to Bridge Street, and Cullen's has taken over Petley's. No.11 has become a tea room and Kingham's has modernised once more. Across the road Gurney's shops are at last flourishing. There are plenty of cars and bicycles to be seen, including the local bobby on his bike.

11.   Several changes had also occurred further up the street, as shown in this photograph of *c*.1930. Outside Stait's a board advertises that *Hook Line and Sinker* is showing at the Embassy, North Harrow. The flowers and tree have gone from Wakefield House where Madame Dussegne, corsetière, is now in business, and a sign of the times is Gurney's motor works further up, where a car is parked on the pavement—true portent of the future. Piercy's at the top has been tricked out with false timbering and turned into a tea shop. The War Memorial is in place and the *Cocoa Tree* has become the Conservative Club.

12.   The building which is now the *Victory* has only been a public house since 1958—before then its use had changed frequently. When this picture was taken *c*.1905 the shed at the end of the side yard was occupied by Tripp's forge, and the present no.2 High Street was under construction, as the scaffolding poles at the extreme right indicate.

23. Woodman's corn chandlery eventually became the very large Woodman's nursery business, occupying four adjacent shops in the High Street. Woodman came to Pinner in the early 1890s and this is his first shop, at no.21. Beside the door is the first notice about Boy Scouts in Pinner.

24. The *Queen's Head* is one of the best known sights in Pinner, though in 1931 the windows were altered and fake timbers were added. It has been an inn since the time of Charles I. The London coach left from here in the 19th century. Early in the 20th, licensee Dawson Billows kept a bear in the stables for about a year, and sometimes took it for a walk.

15. Wilson & Rackliff were jobmasters with stables behind the *Queen's Head*. They would meet you at the station if given notice, or take your daughter and guests to her wedding. Smart young Wally Rackliff shows off the fine service available.

16. Peters' distinctively shaped delivery cart poses outside the shop, and the miller's van and another rig get in on the act, together with other locals. Peters' was one of a succession of bakers and confectioners at 33 High Street where the bread was baked on the premises and sold by weight. Children liked the shop because they were often given jam tarts when mother paid the weekly bill.

17. Mr. and Mrs. George Fuller (at the top of the High Street next to Odell) display their stock. The year is about 1930, and the month obviously June or July because there are peas and broad beans in the baskets at the front and cherries in a window basket.

18.   Frederick Gurney's Central Stores at 38-40 High Street, early this century, with fruit and vegetables, sides of bacon, tinned goods and alcohol much in evidence. The owner stands on the step flanked by six shopmen, two other employees and a young man in a suit, probably the manager of the off-licence. The business was considered high class and was obviously substantial.

19. Harry Lines, *c*.1900, at the door of 34-36 High Street where he set up his business in 1883. The round objects are wheel rims, and lads would sometimes set them rolling down the hill before running off. After the First World War the shop was moved to no.26 where the Lines family continue as decorators' merchants.

20. Shirvell's Coffee and Dining Rooms, newsagent and stationery shop at no.32 photographed in June 1900, the elegant Georgian house quite hidden by adverts. You could also place orders for boot repairs here, or book-binding and printing, or hire a lock-up for your cycle. Eight newspapers are advertised—*Daily News*, *Daily Telegraph*, *Standard*, *Daily Mail*, *London Daily Chronicle*, *Express*, *Lloyds News*, and *Pinner Observer*, and the hot news was the imminent collapse of the Boers at Pretoria.

21. Here is the wonderful front of Shirvell's other shop at no.24 High Street. This would be expensive stuff to leave outside, so it may have been a special display. The hat hanging by the door looks as though it has holes in it for horse or donkey ears.

NEY & HILSDEN.
LATE W. PENDRY.
RS & CO GENERAL SMITHS.

KS

22.   Bridge Street in 1902 is almost unrecognisable. Behind the wall at the right stood Howard Place, built as an almshouse for the widows of clergy and officers. Just beyond the trees is Woodland Cottage, and above that peeps out the timbered gable of the police station, the only thing in the picture which survives today. A building society and a florist (nos.27-29) now stand on the site of the left-hand villas.

23.   Within a few years, the garden of Howard Place was replaced by this row of shops which marked a major expansion of shopping facilities in Pinner. On the opposite side of the road was an assortment of cottages—the small white cottages of Henry Hedges, beyond them The Cottage, of brick, and Dears Farm at the top.

24.   By 1935 Dears Farm was the last but one of those old houses to survive, indicating the former street frontage. A new and lofty range of shops on both sides of the road includes branches of many new chain stores—Sainsbury just above Salmon's lorry, then Boots, Mac Fisheries and Dewhurst. The building with a hipped roof at the end of the shops is the present post office. Almost every form of transport is represented—car, van, lorry, trike, bike, bus and horse-cart, few of them actually moving.

25. Dears Farm was a fine old timber-framed building prominently positioned at the top of Bridge Street. By the 20th century it was in multiple occupation and no longer a farm. The Parslows lived in the white part, and the Pendrys at the left. Pendry was a carman (transporter) who used the yard at the side for his business. The photograph was taken in February 1935, shortly before demolition.

26. Here is young Mrs. Parslow.

27. Mrs. Parslow's three 'Just Williams' (Herbert, Wilfred—seated—and Ernest).

28. This close-up of The Cottage, which also appears in no.24, was taken *c*.1910 when it seems to have been a shop. At the door, with a grandchild perhaps, is Mrs. Rackliff, whose husband ran the *Oddfellows* opposite.

29. There are several significant elements in this photograph. The Cottage was the last of the old properties at the top of Bridge Street to go, after which the whole street line could be set back. The new post office is mostly hidden because of the camera angle. Alongside it looms that essential feature of the 1930s, the local cinema, The Langham, opened in 1936, taking the place of Dears Farm. The cinema was replaced by a supermarket in the 1980s.

30. Adjoining The Cottage at the left was this row of three timber and plaster cottages, once owned by Henry Hedges, probably put up cheaply in the 18th century, and knocked down in the mid-1930s. Even at that date there were many families living in similar and even older houses in Pinner. Some had acquired the amenity of a cold tap in the house, but others had outside stand-pipes and certainly outside toilets, right up to the time of demolition.

31. Hayden House, built as a yeoman's house about 1600, stood a little further down Bridge Street and well back. For a long time it was owned by a local farming family named Hill, until they sold it in 1889 to the sitting tenant, Miss Charlotte Hayden, who named it after her family. The last occupiers were her nephew Joseph Perry, together with her brother-in-law, William Pask, a blind basket-maker whom people tended to remember well. It was another casualty of the 1930s.

32. This is the only known picture of the Waxwell Bakery, actually in Bridge Street, built in very plain style on the plot in front of Hayden House in 1898. It was remembered chiefly as Frank Smith's bakery. Today's bakery, Wenzel's, is on the same spot.

33. A view in Bridge Street looking towards High Street in the snow of 1961 or 1962. The bus, no.183, is resting outside the *Red Lion* before setting off. This was a terminus for buses, made possible by the broad turning space afforded at the junction of the wide end of Bridge Street with Love Lane. This width probably owed its origin to the space needed to ford the river Pinn.

34. The *Red Lion* lasted from some time in the 18th century until it was replaced by Red Lion Parade in 1963. The version seen here was built in 1875. The Pinner fire brigade was manned by part-time volunteers, and was a source of great pride to its members and the village. This looks like a parade rather than a call out. The man with white whiskers behind the driver is Thomas Rayner (*see* no.158).

35.   This is the view from the *Red Lion* across Bridge Street to Chapel Lane, *c*.1900. The 19th-century wooden cottages in front of the railway embankment were demolished in 1942, and to their left, at the other side of the bridge over the river, is the former village school building of 1841, knocked down in 1966. The row of shops at the corner of Chapel Lane, the first ones to appear in Bridge Street *c*.1870, included two sweet shops, which accounts for the attention of the children. Between them is a butcher's shop shaded by a wooden canopy.

36.   The butcher's shop belonged to George Hedges, the man with the white beard, with George junior beside him. This photograph of about 1890 is probably a specially posed scene, perhaps upon a fresh delivery from Smithfield. George senior grew up at East End Farm.

37.   All that remains of this 1924 view of Chapel Lane is the railway bridge, later rebuilt and widened, and the house behind the garden wall at the left. The wooden cottages on the left, seen on the previous page, housed small tradesmen like Aslin the boot repairer. The shop at the other side with a corner door is Brewster's, newsagent, tobacconist and confectioner. Along the lane are three little cottages dating from the early 17th century, in one of which the first Methodist services in Pinner were held. Their site is now partly within Woolworth's back yard, and SupaSnaps covers Brewster's.

38.   In the lean-to of the 17th-century cottage in Chapel Lane was Page's very small butcher's shop, and here in 1906 is Tom, sharpening his knife and looking ready for business. Without a traditional shop front one wonders about the adequacy of the premises, even though the building was probably not quite as old as that of John Lee, the butcher in High Street.

39.   The house behind the garden wall in Chapel Lane was built as a pair *c*.1840. The wall has gone and many people remember the place as a charity shop. In 1985-6 it was very much enlarged, and re-opened as Chapel Lane Chambers, offering estate agent and associated services.

40.   This is a scene by Pinner bridge at the foot of the High Street, *c*.1900, with a crowd attracted by what is said to have been the first motor car seen in the village. The man on his own at the left is James Bedford, parish clerk. Everything here has been renewed, even the bridge; the hall beside the bridge went in 1966; the bank site at the corner was taken over and rebuilt by Barclays in 1902, though the premises are now used by estate agents; the *Victory* public house next door has made way for a private car park, and an office block replaced the adjoining houses in 1985.

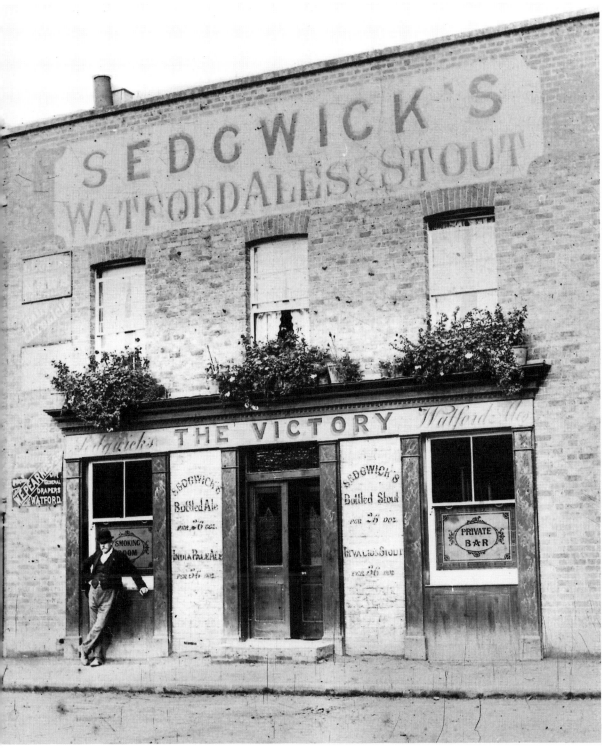

41. Charles Greenfield stands outside the *Victory* in Marsh Road at the beginning of this century, the epitome of the ordinary Edwardian man. His father-in-law, Daniel Rayner, had been licensee from 1873-1888. The *Victory* shifted to no.4 High Street in 1958 and the old pub was knocked down to provide rear access to it. Charles lived in one of the old cottages near the top of Bridge street (*see* no.30), and was the head gardener at West House (*see* no.92).

42.   In this view from Marsh Road to Bridge Street, taken about 1902, the *Victory* is just off to the right. The buildings across the river were replaced by a row of shops in 1933, while beyond them at the far side of Love Lane is the garden of Howard Place. At the left the High Street Gardens occupy the sites of the shop and the parish hall, which had served as the first National School from when it was built in 1841 until 1866.

43.   Marsh Road *c.*1910 looks incredibly peaceful (although the school was just behind the chapel), as the shoveller collects useful droppings for his garden. The chapel was built by Thomas Grimwood in 1885 to replace the Baptist Chapel driven out of Chapel Lane by the railway. Cecil Park has been laid out to the right, and soon Stanley Villas will be built at its left. The chapel became Pinner's first synagogue in 1941, and was rebuilt in 1981.

44.   Cecil Park was an early venture by the Metropolitan Railway Surplus Lands Company to exploit its unused land, and had its own direct entrance to Pinner station. Begun in 1900, the road was not completed until the 1930s. This is the first pair of houses, nos.18-24.

45.   The second National School building, with its fancy brickwork, was tucked behind the early 19th-century Lichfield's Cottage facing Marsh Road in 1866, and a new lane was made for access. The stacked bricks were probably being used to build Stanley Villas at the west of School Lane, and the house made way for the additional terrace built in front of the school in 1914. The Baptist Chapel can be seen in the background on the right.

46.   These were some of the National School boys in 1902. In the centre is Charles Grenside, vicar of Pinner from 1886-1910, who began the parish magazine, and was the first local historian of Pinner. On his immediate right is Edwin Ware, later the parish clerk and Pinner's most notable local historian. The headmaster, Charles Billows, stands at the extreme left and his assistant, William King, on the right.

47.   Several early 19th-century wooden cottages stood in Marsh Road opposite Stanley Villas. This pair stood by the footpath between the Memorial Park and West End Avenue; the river flowed between Marsh Road and the cottages and the little bridge served them and the footpath. They survived until the 1930s.

48.   Here is Marsh Road during the 1940s. Stanley Villas at the left have been converted to shops, and the shopping parade of 1937 has raised the skyline. The wooden cottages which were behind the trees at the right have gone and the late 19th-century brick cottages were soon to go too.

49.   Marsh Road outside the library on 17 August 1977 after a torrential downpour, a scene repeated elsewhere along the course of the Pinn. In medieval times, when the water table was higher, flooding may have been more frequent, and so it is not surprising that this end of the village was called the Marsh.

50. Pinner Place fronted onto Marsh Road until it was knocked down in 1954 and replaced by Ashridge Gardens. This early 18th-century rebuilding of an older house was one of Pinner's mansions, lived in at the end of the century by John Zephaniah Holwell, survivor of the Black Hole of Calcutta, and the crown jeweller James Garrard in the last decades of the 19th century. It was used as a hospital for war-wounded during the First World War (*see* no.171).

51. This is the entrance hall of Pinner Place as it looked at the turn of the century, possibly in the time of Garrard, redolent of a wealthy way of life. The palm may have been brought on in the hot house or conservatory, which was a customary adjunct to a house of this kind.

52.   Melrose Road, at the right, and Kingsley Road to the left were built on a green field site *c*.1911, rows of small but solid houses. They were at the edge of Pinner, which probably accounts for the provision of a shop, originally a grocer's shop. In these days it is superfluous, and shut.

53.   Pinner station in January 1934 looked much as it did when it was opened on 25 May 1885—although by 1934 the porch had been removed and the chimneys shortened. This is the 'up' platform. The first service ran every thirty minutes to Baker Street. Plans to rebuild the station with an entrance in Marsh Road were withered by the Second World War.

54.   Pinner signal box with its staff, c.1910. In the background are the contractor's huts for the building of Cecil Park, whose first few houses are already up, including nos.18-24 at the left (see no. 44).

55. The horse-drawn bus service, begun by the London & North Western Railway when the rival station was opened by the Metropolitan Railway in 1885, ran for almost thirty years, taking a variable route between the village and the main line station at Hatch End. George Bridge (shown here) drove it for most of that time. Four passengers could travel inside, paying 4d.(2p) for a complete single journey.

56. In 1914 a motor bus service from Harrow was extended to Pinner. More routes were introduced as building progressed, including the still surviving no.183. Route 181B of the London General Omnibus Company, shown here, ran between the *Red Lion* and Uxbridge from 1932, and was renumbered 220 in 1934. Route 208 left from here to go to the top of Pinner Hill but lasted only a year—the journey, similar in length to that of the old horse bus, cost 3d.(1.25p).

57. The installation of a further pair of rail tracks was completed in June 1961, enabling fast trains to by-pass the station, and the 'down' platform was rebuilt at the same time. The railway sidings and goods yard at the right were to remain in use for another six years. They had been more extensive between the wars when they were used to bring in building materials, and domestic coal for retail by the merchants with offices in Station Approach.

58.   Pinner House in Church Lane, whose slightly asymmetrical Queen Anne façade may cover an older house, is one of the few mansions to survive. The incumbent of Pinner could afford to live in it at the end of the 18th century. In the 19th it was bought by Jason Woodbridge, whose family had made its money in the local building trade. Since 1947 it has provided accommodation for the elderly. This view of 1978 shows the individual flats recently completed at the rear, and sun-shaded tables at the front for the use of the residents.

9. Mount Cottage, dating from the 1830s, was the precursor of the house called Blackgates. In the middle of the 19th century Miss Caroline Doogood kept her school here, with 16 resident children aged between four and ten years of age recorded in 1851.

0. Benjamin Weall retired rom farming and built Rugby House in Church Lane c.1855 with bricks said to have come rom Rugby. Most of the grounds were sold to the Metropolitan Railway Company in 1885, etaining for the resident of The Grange, as the house was soon alled, a private short cut from he garden to the station. The company's development of its and in the 20th century put an nd to this scene of 1896 south f the house. The building is now ubdivided into The Grange and Rugby House.

61. There have been some changes at the east end of Church Lane since this view was taken *c*.1892. The house at the right has been divided into two, Mulberry Cottage and the Bay House, and Grange Gardens runs from the lane along the side of Grange Cottage, which at this date housed the gardener of The Grange. The low building beyond Grange Cottage is said to have been a sheep shed. Elmdene, in the distance, had been a farmhouse many years before, part of the old hamlet of Nower Hill.

62. One of the first residents of Elmdene after it had ceased to be a farmhouse was Horatia, the natural daughter of Lord Nelson and Lady Hamilton. She was the widow of the Rev. Philip Ward of Tenterden when she came to Pinner, where one of her sons already lived. She died in 1881 and lies in Paines Lane Cemetery. In this photograph her resemblance to her father is striking (*see* no.93).

63.   The granite fountain on Nower Hill Green, nucleus of the medieval hamlet of Nower Hill, commemorates the generosity of William Tooke in restoring the parish church in 1880. Nowadays the green, fully surrounded by houses, is sometimes called Tooke's Green. At the left is the old Nower Hill House, on a site at the corner of Wakehams Hill which had been occupied since medieval times. The picture dates from about 1900.

64.   Ambrose Heal, of the Tottenham Court Road store, bought the old Nower Hill House soon after his son of the same name had moved into Pinner, and had it brought up to date and altered to the newest style by the architect Cecil Brewer. The family stayed until 1940, and Mrs. Heal's collection of local memorabilia is in the local history library.

65. In 1900 Cecil Brewer designed The Fives Court for the younger Ambrose Heal, very much in the style of the nowadays better known Charles Voysey. This view shows it before it was extended in 1910. At the back it had a small court for the game of fives, hence the name of the house.

66. Ambrose Heal the younger at the gate of The Fives Court, c.1910.

67.   East House was one of the old timber-framed houses of the hamlet at East End in Moss Lane. It had been modernised and enlarged long before this picture was taken in the 1930s when it belonged to Edward Montesole, a local and county councillor who was instrumental in securing the establishment of the green belt. East Glade now crosses the site.

68.   Chiswick House had formerly been known as Terrilands, and marked the site of another medieval house at East End. It was a nursing home when Dr. Macaulay was there in the 1930s. After demolition in 1964 it was replaced by Chiswick Court and Bloomsbury Court.

69. East End House hides behind its hedge, a house of mixed dates and appearance. Its most notable resident was one of the least regarded poets laureate, Henry James Pye, whose work has been out of print since shortly after his death in 1813. This was his home for the last three years of his life. There is a memorial to him above the south door of the church.

70. East End Farm Cottage is one of Pinner's oldest houses, dating from the late 15th century. It began life as the home of a yeoman farmer, and remained a farmhouse until the middle of the 1930s. At that time it was in the hands of the Hedges family, who had been resident for about a hundred years. A partly consumed hayrick is visible behind the house in this early 20th-century photograph.

71. This is Martha, wife of William Hedges who worked East End Farm from 1840 until 1881, and was the first of three generations there. Both of them had been born in 1815, the year of the battle of Waterloo, and Martha survived William by 12 years. George Hedges, the butcher, was their second son (*see* no.36).

72. Mosslane Cottage is a survivor of the former hamlet of Bury Pond, portions of it dating from the early 17th century. The left-hand part is the older, and was originally the rear of the house, before the road was re-aligned to go so close to it. The part at the right was added in 1887 by William Barber of Barrow Point House. The cottage was divided into two residences in 1951.

73.   Barrow Point House was, until 1890, the residence of William Barber, a judge who was energetic in local affairs (*see* no.4). After his death in 1891 his trustees began selling off parts of the large estate for development. In this photograph of 1913 the girls seem to be making a mess of one of the heaps of newly mown grass. The lady with the bow beneath her chin is Mrs. Edwin Ware (*see* no.7).

74.   St John's Preparatory School, begun in Pinner vicarage and directed by Mr. Norman, took over Barrow Point House which was altered and enlarged. The school moved to Potter Street Hill in 1970 and the house has been replaced by the flats and cottages known as Barrowdene Close.

75.   This terrace of four cottages, which used to stand near the river in Paines Lane, on the site of the present nos.91-93, was demolished in 1939, having lasted about a century. They were the homes of labourers and artisans. John Dell's family lived in one for over forty years, and Joseph, one of his sons, moved into another one when he acquired his own family.

76.   At Rockstone House in Paines Lane lived Janie Terrero, one of Pinner's most militant suffragettes. An accomplished middle-class English lady, married to an Argentinian, she was imprisoned for four months in 1912 for having broken windows in Regent Street while participating in a demonstration. The large house and garden, no.77 Paines Lane, has been replaced.

77.   A section of Love Lane before any development, between The Avenue, which did not yet exist, and Waxwell Lane. The three gentlemen of the road have been interrupted in their tea-making. The photograph was taken in the early 1890s by a member of the Beaumont family, to which the two lads may belong.

78.   Here is Love Lane, *c.*1910, when the west side had been built up, but not the eastern. The van must be delivering goods, which was typical in those days, even if the shop were just around the corner. It is also very likely that many of these houses, which still stand, had a resident servant, occupying a room in the attic. A few years later the plot behind the fence at the right was taken up by the Methodists.

79.   The Bridge Street end of Love Lane in 1903. In the distance is Wilby House, removed to make way for the car park entrance, and beside it an old cottage replaced by maisonettes in the 1950s. The horse bus has just passed the garden of Howard Place at the left, where two little children with a go-cart seem to have caught sight of the camera. The proper subjects of the picture are standing in front of the fire station at the side of the *Red Lion*.

80.   The first church of St Luke was built in 1915 next to Howard Place, and in a side chapel the national shrine to St Philomena (a Roman martyr canonised in the 19th century) was established in 1931. It was transferred to the new church, built on the site of Howard Place in 1957, but declined when the cult was officially suppressed in 1960. The old church has been adapted as parish rooms. The picture shows the first shrine, including the still-existing small window (in the left wall of the alcove) designed by the stained-glass artist Francis Humphreys of Cannon Lane (*see* no.103).

81.   This well-head can still be seen at the top of Waxwell Lane, the 19th-century remnant of the medieval well of the same name. The pump which eliminated hauling was set up at the back in the 19th century and last used about a decade before this photograph was taken in 1910. The road in the background is Uxbridge Road and the cottages are nos.546-48 at the corner of Blythwood Road.

82. Waxwell Farm was the house of a 17th-century yeoman. In 1947 it was acquired by The Grail, a Roman Catholic organisation which uses it as an ecumenical centre and has provided a chapel, conference hall, and residential facilities. Until 1991 a public garden party was held every summer, which is the activity going on in the illustration. This rear wing of the house was added at the end of the 19th century, but a tiny piece of the old part can be seen at the right.

83. The 16th-century Orchard Cottage, in Waxwell Lane near the police station, pictured *c*.1920. The stables and plot alongside were used as a council depot. The building further up the lane is Bee Cottage, of a similar date.

Waxwell Lane, Pinner

84. The single-storey house is no.31 Waxwell Lane when it was the hall of the Manchester Unity of Oddfellows. The Pinner Lodge was inaugurated in 1845, and this meeting room was built in 1866, as well as the two cottages alongside to bring in revenue—they were called, appropriately, Manchester Villas. The Pinner Lodge has been wound up, and at the time of writing the hall is being converted into a matching two-storeyed cottage.

85. Thomas Ellement in his regalia as Noble Grand of the British Queen Lodge of the Manchester Unity of Oddfellows in Pinner, which he founded, and served until his death in 1899 at the age of 79. By trade he was a carpenter and joiner, and was the building manager for many of the ventures of Arthur Tooke of Pinner Hill. The Ellement family was active in Pinner affairs, and some members are still in business as funeral directors.

86. This must be one of the oldest photographs of Pinner, showing the *Oddfellows Arms* in 1860, before any extensions. The right end of the frontage has no garden because of the delivery hatch. The public house was built in 1854 by Thomas Ellement, who also held the licence.

87. By 1913, the probable date of this picture, the garden of the pub had been built over. The gabled house is Pinner police station, built in 1899, excellently placed to keep an eye on the conduct of the drinkers opposite. The stable for the sergeant's horse still stands at the back.

88. Here in his robes is Sir Ernest Jelf, the King's Remembrancer, whose duties included presiding over the testing of gold and silver coinage at the annual Trial of the Pyx, and wearing in the Lord Mayor of London. Sir Ernest lived in Pinner for over 50 years, at no.688 Pinner Road, Church Farm, and St Mary's Cottage in Waxwell Lane.

89. This is Brassy Baker with his horse and dustcart at the council depot in Waxwell Lane early in the 1930s, when Pinner was still part of Hendon Rural District. Brassy earned his nickname by constantly burnishing the horse brasses.

90. The nearer of these buildings in Elm Park Road the First Church of Christ Scientist, erected in 1937. Before that the Scientists met in the Oddfellows Hall, and then in temporary accommodation on the plot. The block of flats is North End Lodge, a good example of the redevelopment in 1965 of the site of a single house, in this case North End Villa, built about a century before.

91.   Tudor Cottage, 13 Elm Park Road was designed in the 1930s by Ernest Trobridge, an idiosyncratic architect who specialised in medieval and Tudor pastiche. It is a listed building and, whereas a few years ago it was surrounded by contemporary but orthodox detached houses, redevelopment has marooned it among town houses and flats of the 1990s.

92. West House replaced one of the old yeomen's houses at the hamlet of West End. Nelson's grandson lived here in the 1870s. It was rebuilt early in the 19th century and subsequently improved until it was a mansion in large and ornamental grounds. It is the only such estate to survive in Pinner—saved by the people of Pinner as a war memorial and renamed Pinner Memorial Park. This view shows house and lake just before the larger part of the house was pulled down in 1950.

93. West Lodge, difficult to see beneath its veil of creeper, looks like a Georgian house with a late 19th-century addition. Its chief claim to fame was as one of the early residences of Nelson's daughter, Horatia. She lived here in the 1860s when it was called Hazelwood. West Lodge School took over its site and name in 1954.

94. This house adjoining the school is used these days for ancillary educational purposes, but it was once West End Farmhouse, a late Victorian replacement of a much older farm. There are still a few former stables at the side, adapted for a milk delivery depot by the United Dairies, which took over between the world wars.

95. William Treneman of Cornwall Cottage in West End Lane was Cornish by name and birth. He was pastor of the Baptist Chapel in Chapel Lane from 1876 to 1880, and remained a deacon. Although born in 1820, he must still have been a man of energy, for he became the school attendance officer, and also married for the third time in 1898, on which occasion he skipped his duties to go on honeymoon.

Situated in the corner of Eastcote Road and West End Lane was yet another large estate, The Towers, residence of Arthur and Bertha Marshall. He was chairman of the Pinner Gas Company further up the road and Captain of the Fire Brigade, and she was a partner in a cookery school in Mortimer Street, London. The last window in the north aisle of St John's Church (designed by Sir Ninian Comper) was Arthur's memorial to her.

97. Nearer the gas works is the terrace called Oak Cottages. There were only four of them when built in 1867 as a speculative venture, with labourers and artisans in mind. Some were occupied by gas workers. A fifth was added in matching style and materials, about 1980. This photograph was taken in 1970.

98. The single-storey hut which housed the Vagabonds' Club was in Eastcote Road near Marsh Road, where the Pinn Medical Centre is now. The club had its origins in a section of the membership of the Pinner Men's Club which broke away from its parent in 1920 and chose the new name to reflect the act. It was a social club for both sexes, and it has been said that many a Pinner romance began here.

99. The *Cocoa Tree* at the top of the High Street was very popular with day trippers, both as individuals and in parties. The proprietor provided facilities for the latter in a field off Eastcote Road where Meadow Road is now. This occasion looks like a Sunday School treat for non-locals—there are donkeys and swing-boats in the background.

100.   Fields around the edge of the village centre were used for other recreational activities. These are the entrants for the mile race at Pinner Village Sports at a time when Pinner was still sufficiently small for such village-wide community events to be possible. Neither winner nor date, which may be about 1912, is known. Standing at the left is Fay Gregory, a footballer with Watford F.C.

101.   The Donkey Derby was an occasional event at the annual garden fête of St Luke's Church, when a number of leading jockeys took part. Following the example of the initiator, Steve Donoghue, the Epsom Derby winner donated his winning boots and a cup. This is the line-up for the 1938 event, which took place in the grounds of The Grove, with Steve Donoghue at the left and Gordon Richards in the middle. Donoghue was the winner.

102. The houses at the northern end of Eastcote Road and Cannon Lane appeared just before the First World War. At what is now no.2 Cannon Lane lived stained-glass designer Francis Humphreys and his brother. Although the house was not large, they were among those people who could afford a resident servant, in their case a housekeeper, who is seen in the study amid an array of Francis' designs.

103. Francis Humphreys in the back garden.

104. This was The Lodge, a very stylish 18th-century house whose site is now covered by Elm Park Court. John Zephaniah Holwell bought the house after his wife's death in 1794 (*see* no.50).

105. Elm Park Court flats were built in 1935, spaciously set around a central garden in an echo of the house they superseded. The mixture of art deco style in the doors, windows and balconies, in the white stucco walls and smooth entrance archway, with the bright green pantiles, is striking even today.

106. Adjoining The Lodge at the West End Lane side was Hazeldene. In this house, or a predecessor, lived John Carel, one of Pinner's first known nurserymen, who in 1818 registered with the Royal Horticultural Society the Pinner Seedling, a dessert apple he had been developing since 1810. A block of flats was built on the site in 1965, and all that remains of The Lodge and Hazeldene is the wall that divided them, seen here on the right.

107. The only recognisable object in this picture is the row of cottages. They still stand, nos.18-50 Pinner Green. The *Starling* is just out of sight around the far corner, and the *Bell*, the old one, is a few yards up behind the trees on the left—the pub was rebuilt at the left hand corner in the 1930s. The lorry, and the fact that the street lamp seems to be blacked out, suggests a date for the picture soon after the First World War.

108. Austin Carley was the licensee of the *Bell* at the end of the last century, and here he is in a pony and trap outside his premises, with farmer James Gregory of Woodhall Farm holding the bridle, *c*.1890. The pony was Flying Fan, whom Gregory, her owner, used to race successfully against other local ponies—and whose hooves he preserved.

109.   Two young ladies pause with their prams in Rickmansworth Road at its junction with Cuckoo Hill and Pinner Green, *c*.1920. The shop was one of the small general stores which grew up to serve outlying locations; it had originated as a front-room shop in no.1 Cuckoo Hill, adjoining. The shop survives, in other hands, and a porch has been added to no.1. Behind the hedge at the right was, and is, the *Starling*, while behind the left one was Ashill Cottage, now replaced by a parade of shops.

110.   Pinner windmill burnt down in 1874, just four years after this picture was painted. In those days it was only grinding animal meal. The buildings are those of Mill Farm, established after the early 19th-century enclosure on what had been Pinner Common. The road at the front is Pinner Hill Road, and the entrance track is more or less where Mill Farm Close has since been laid out.

111. Almost opposite the mill was this row of eight wooden cottages, only one storey high. They were built in the 1830s and, as they were once called Coronation Cottages, the year of Queen Victoria's anointing is probably the right one. Their colloquial name was the Rabbit Hutches. The photograph shows an assortment of resident children in 1919. The cottages were demolished in 1926.

112. These council houses of the late 1920s or 1930s were on the western side of Pinner Hill Road. The mock Tudor effect is a little unusual for municipal stock, but was associated with the experimental nature of the materials used, asbestos and timber. Within a few years they were leaking badly. After the Second World War they were condemned, and were pulled down in 1968 to be replaced by flats.

113. It is difficult to sort out the architectural history of the house called Antoneys, of which this is the only known picture. Much of it was reconstructed after a serious fire in 1893. The most notable resident of this particular Pinner mansion was Sir Frank Ree, general manager of the former London and North Western Railway which ran through Hatch End. After the house was demolished in 1952 the estate was filled with a good mixture of council flats, bungalows and cottages set among the large number of trees and shrubs which were retained.

114. As with many places in Pinner, the Dingles, shown here in 1908, was a descendant of earlier houses on the site. Although situated in Uxbridge Road, it was known for most of the 19th century as Waxwell House. By 1931 it housed Meriston House School, then The Knoll School. It was replaced, inevitably, by a block of flats called The Knoll.

115.   Waxwell House was acquired by Thomas Thompson about 1837, and here is his grandson, George Thompson, who was born at the house in 1866, balancing on a penny-farthing—probably with the support of the garden wall. He designed stained glass windows with C. E. Kempe.

116.   The northern area of Pinner had a high concentration of grand houses, and The Hall, sometimes called The Old Hall, was at the corner of Paines Lane and Uxbridge Road. It was a Georgian house modernised in the 1870s by George Bird, a building contractor who had made his fortune in Kensington and Paddington. His daughter Jessie married Nelson Ward, grandson of the hero of Trafalgar.

117.   The main entrance to The Hall was in Uxbridge Road, complete with gate and lodge. Although the house has gone the lodge remains, somewhat enlarged, at the corner of the drive to the house, which is now called Old Hall Drive. In this bucolic scene of the early 20th century it is still a lodge and Uxbridge Road had not begun to fill with houses.

118. The Hall had an ornamental lake, like many of Pinner's mansions, but this one figures in several reminiscences because people were sometimes allowed to skate on it when it was frozen over. Here is just such a scene, apparently Edwardian. Ernest Jelf (*see* no.88) is at the far top left, while the man in the pale jersey is the local newsagent, G. Jaques. It was west of the bridge in Old Hall Drive.

119. In 1844 Pinner Hill House, now the clubhouse of Pinner Hill Golf Club, became the home of Arthur Tooke, who could afford to indulge his taste for Victorian Gothic architecture (*see* nos.120, 123, 124, 127). The new front he added to this house can be glimpsed at the left behind the 18th-century rear façade, which looks eastward over the golf course. When the Dore family owned the estate, Stanley Baldwin and W. S. Gilbert were visitors. The golf club was established on part of the estate in 1927, while the rest of it was gradually built upon.

20. Tooke's additions included an unusual clock tower set in the garden in 1869. The clock itself had been made in 1846, and the quarter hours were rung on five bells which had been made in Moscow and bought by Tooke at the Great Exhibition of 1851 in Hyde Park. The tower and its associated buildings were demolished in 1962—by which time the bells had vanished.

21. One of the expensive new houses to arise on Pinner Hill in 1936 was the present Sans Souci in South View Road. It is said to have been commissioned by Joachim von Ribbentrop whilst he was German ambassador to Britain, and constructed of narrow red bricks brought from Germany. The interior still has most of its original art deco fittings. In 1938 it was acquired by the sister of Hermann Goering, the German finance minister.

122. This is the view of Pinner Hill farmhouse and yard, perhaps in the late 1940s, taken from the top of the tower (*see below*). It had been the home farm of the Pinner Hill estate, and James Gregory (*see* no.108) was its last farmer. Beside the house was a small chalk mine. In recent times horses were stabled here, but now a new use has been found by converting the stables and sheds around the yard into dwellings.

123. The tower at Pinner Hill Farm, the only one of the three ornamental ones built by Arthur Tooke which still stands, was built as part of a stable but has now been turned into offices. This view shows the north face before the restoration and conversion.

124.   Pinnerwood Farm was also a creation of Arthur Tooke, almost a gingerbread house. It was tenanted at one time by the Gregorys (*see* no.108). Today it is a stud farm.

125. Woodhall Farm began as a large estate belonging to the lord of the manor, but is now no more than a private house. It was given this appearance about 1810 when John C. Loudon and his father William held the tenancy. The taller wing was added by them. They had great plans for modernising farming methods, but William's death cut short the process.

126. This is a rare picture of Woodhall Towers in its street setting—an interloper, it seems, among the neat and traditional houses of the Pinnerwood Park Estate. They, however, were the newcomers.

127.   Woodhall Towers was an extravagant house built by Arthur Tooke. It was exciting to look at, and attracted the local epithet of Tooke's Folly, although whether this was a comment on its appearance or its practicability as a dwelling is not known. For a year or two around 1931 it was used as an hotel. It was demolished in 1965—had it survived, it would probably now be regarded as having architectural importance.

128. Burnt Oak Farm was established at the northern end of Oxhey Lane in the early 19th century, taking its name from a boundary oak nearby. The photograph was taken in 1972, not long before demolition, although one barn has survived. The oak went in 1938.

129. Little is known of Oxhey Lane Farm, almost opposite, even though there has been one here close to the county boundary for centuries. It has always been relatively isolated. Because it is in the green belt it has been able to continue as a farm, despite being cut in two by the railway line, but at the time of writing agricultural policies have jeopardised its dairy business and it seeks to diversify. The picture was taken in 1972.

130. Here is the heart of the original hamlet of Hatch End, although the oldest buildings to be seen here are the two terraces of cottages at the left, separated by the *Letchford Arms*, all built in the 1870s by the owner of Hatch End Farm. The pub was altered in 1928. The cottage nearest the camera was a shop. The houses at the right are early 20th-century houses built in a traditional cottage style, to which more have been added. Just out of sight beyond the end terrace is the oldest house in Hatch End, the 17th-century Letchford House, which used to be Hatch End Farm.

131. A small corner of the earlier Hatch End station (originally called Pinner) can just be seen behind the building in the foreground. It was rebuilt in neo-Georgian style in 1911 to the design of Gerald Horsley, who also redesigned Harrow & Wealdstone station. The building with the chimney is the station master's house, and the post office occupies the single-storey extension nearer the camera. A telegraph boy stands inside the gate with his bicycle.

132.   Dove House was another Pinner mansion to vanish beneath high-rise development, commemorated in the name of the Dove House flats which ousted it. This is the rear which looked southward over the gardens. Early in the 19th century it was rented by John Tilbury, who invented the 'tilbury' carriage. There was a house here in medieval times—in the 16th century a dovecote was one of the appurtenances, and the name followed.

133.   Woodridings Farm was where Woodridings Close joins Uxbridge Road and, like most others locally, it prospered as a dairy farm at the start of the 20th century. The milk carts of J. & S. Mordin, who were here during the Edwardian period when milk was delivered to the customer straight from the churn, are lined up for the camera, c.1908. The farm produced its own Pinner Lactic Cheese, which did well enough to be taken over by the St. Ivel Company.

134. This is how Uxbridge Road appeared early this century, looking westward from Wellington Road, and showing some of the houses on the Woodridings Estate. The further one was called Woodridings and looked the same as 2 Chandos Villas. The nearer house was called Littlecote.

135. The first residents of 2 Chandos Villas, Woodridings were Samuel Beeton and his bride Isabella. It was here that she wrote her famous book on household management, which her husband's employer, Ward Lock, first published in instalments. They left Pinner soon after the recipes were published complete in a single volume.

136.   The *Railway Tavern* was the only commercial enterprise on the Woodridings estate. This must be how it looked at first, except for the bay windows, which were added later. This photograph is probably of the 20th century since there is a little shop at one side. In recent years the bay windows have been removed and the façade simplified. To the right is a glimpse of one of the original pairs of villas, initially called Oak Villas.

137.   The Commercial Travellers' School was one of the first buildings to go up at Hatch End after the station had opened. Boys and girls were kept separate, and it seems from this photograph that they had to keep more than a fence-width apart. The word Royal was added in 1919. After the school had closed down, this building was demolished and the rest used for the Hatch End College of Further Education for a couple of decades, and then for the Harrow Arts Council.

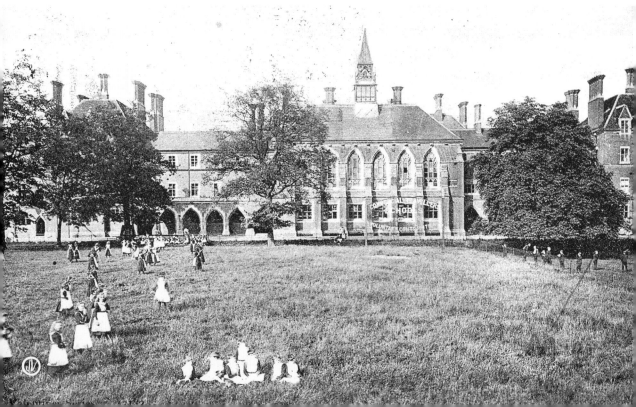

138.   The solid-looking Clonard was built in Oxhey Lane by Sir Alexander Miller, K.C. in the 1890s. By 1912 the Convent of the Immaculate Conception of Our Lady of Lourdes Girls' School had moved from Royston Park Avenue into the neighbouring house called Oxhey Rise, and about 1930 it acquired Clonard, staying until the house was demolished in 1968 and the school was closed. Roman Catholics in the area attended mass in the convent chapel before the church of St Theresa was opened in 1955.

139.   St Anselm's church was founded in 1894 because the temporary church of All Saints' in Wellington Road had become too small. In 1902 there was controversy far beyond Pinner when the rood screen was installed—some people thought it would encourage idolatry. This photograph dates from soon after the north aisle was added in 1906.

140. The houses on the Westfield Park and Royston Park estates around and north of the station are large, and many have been subdivided or redeveloped. They show a wide variety of styles, reflecting an individual approach to the construction of each road of houses. Virginia Lodge in Royston Grove was built by Heinz & Co. in 1924 for the chairman of its English company, Charles Hellen, who came from Maryland, a factor which is thought to account for its slightly southern states colonial appearance.

141. This is Headstone Manor House soon after 1925, when it ceased to be a farm—the yard was no longer in use and barns out of the picture were about to be demolished. The whole of the house to the right of the chimney dates from 1344, and is currently awaiting restoration. The great barn on the left was restored in 1972 and, together with the house, forms the Harrow Museum & Heritage Centre. The white railing is part of the bridge across the moat.

142.   In 1878 George Champness built a cottage right out in the fields at the junction of Harrow View and the present Headstone Gardens, naming it Selina's Retreat, after his wife. They had a milk delivery round (though whether they produced the milk is not clear) and most of their customers were perhaps in the thirty or so small houses which went up around the Kodak works towards the end of the century. Here is George with his daughter-in-law about 1905.

143. The temporary corrugated iron church of St George was erected in 1907 at the corner of Hide Road and Pinner View to serve the rapidly growing western outskirts of Harrow, which at this point overspilled into what had been the Headstone Manor estate in Pinner. The permanent red-brick church was built in 1911 in the intervening space between this one and Longley Road, which is visible in the background.

144. Pinner Park Farm bottles and delivers its milk locally. In this photograph of perhaps the 1960s churns stand on the loading bay of the bottling plant at the right, while a horse rests from its round. The house was built in the 1750s to replace an earlier moated one on a nearby spot, and the taller right-hand wing was added some sixty years later. The large structure at the left is a granary of c.1800 which became obsolete and was transferred to the Heritage Centre at Headstone Manor in 1991.

145. White Cottage, just within the boundary of Pinner Park where the footpath meets Wakehams Hill —a favourite local viewpoint—may have been built as a lodge to watch the gate and stile. There used to be another pathway, leading across the fields to Headstone, which is visible at the right in this picture of 1938. During the later 19th century the resident for many years was George Wakeham, a cobbler. The cottage was demolished in 1971.

146.   Threshing the crops at Pinner Park Farm in 1950.

147.   Imperial Drive in the course of construction about 1926 with the contractor's site railway clearly in evidence. The station is North Harrow, opened in 1915, and the ticket office and steps to the platforms are on the left.

148.   The same view eight years later, at the evening rush hour. The bridge was originally built to allow farm access beneath and the roadway had to be lowered to allow traffic to pass under—a severe storm sometimes causes flooding. The shop at the right, Ellington's, was one of a local chain of newsagents.

149.   The shopping centre along Pinner Road to the north of the station, as it was in 1929 before shops had spread beyond Woodlands at the rear left. Even in this small scene major commercial chains are well represented with an Express Dairy and a National Provincial Bank but pride of place goes to the Embassy Cinema between them. The film showing is *Dynamite*, a melodrama starring Kaye Johnson and Charles Bickford. The cinema closed in 1963 and was replaced by a supermarket and bowling alley.

150. This view of Southfield Park (foreground) and Pinner Road in 1921 shows the streets thrusting out into the countryside. There are already contractor's huts, equipment and pathways in the field adjoining the upper line of houses. The field at the top with its half-used haystack was part of Hope Farm, tenanted by George Barter, whose farmhouse stood to the west of the present junction of Pinner Road and South Way.

151.   Local enthusiasts join the workers and bowler-hatted foreman to watch anxiously as the first 'down' train passes over the new bridge at North Harrow on the morning of 17 November 1929.

On the RIDGEWAY ESTATE & PINNER VILLAGE ESTATE

(Adjoining Pinner's New Public Park)

Type "F"   £795 FREEHOLD

Three-Bedroom type House.   Semi-detached.

Thoroughly Labour-Saving, Brick-Built, of the same quality and containing the same accommodation as Type J, but slightly larger.

ACCOMMODATION :

Wide Entrance Hall.	Three Bedrooms.
Dining Room.	Bathroom,
Drawing Room.	Separate W.C., etc.
Kitchen	

Space for Garage at side of House.

The two Reception Rooms and two Principal Bedrooms are fitted with the latest type hearth fires and tiled surrounds. Tiled Kitchen (with tiled floor) fitted with Enamelled H.W. Boiler, closed-in Dresser, Gas Copper, etc., etc. Bath enclosed in marbled panelling. Decorations carried out, and Shelves and Cupboards fitted.

Gas, Water and Electricity laid on. Gas points to all rooms.

Cash Down	...	...	...	...	£25
On Completion	...	...	...	...	£55
Total Deposit	...	...	...	...	£80
Building Society Mortgage		...	...	...	£715
					£795

Repayments (reduced terms) average per week £1 1s.2d. Rates 9/2 in the £1 for the year. Net assessment approx. £29 p.a.

NO ROAD CHARGES OR LAW COSTS.

"Your Own House is the Best of all Houses"

—An Old Roman Proverb

152. Several builders were involved in the North Harrow area, one of the biggest being the local firm of Cutler, whose first work was done in Hide Road before the First World War. Many of their houses, detached or semi-detached, feature four diamond-set tiles on the façade, and have front doors and landing windows fitted with highly picturesque scenes in coloured glass.

153.   Downs Farmhouse stood in Cannon Lane with its front, seen here, facing east, and its back to the lane. The farm originated towards the middle of the 19th century but about a century later inter-war expansion put an end to the farming. The Methodists bought the site in 1956 and the buildings were gradually replaced by church premises over the next twenty years.

154.   The mixed nature of the stock at Downs Farm is shown in this early 20th-century photograph. The farmer was Joseph Gurney, who was also a coal merchant, assistant overseer, collector of rates, and clerk to the Parish Council. It is not known whether the man in the picture is Gurney.

155.   No.3 Nursery Cottages is the oldest surviving building in Cannon Lane and was provided for the foreman of the sewage farm established at the southern end of the lane in 1880. Roxbourne Park Recreation Ground superseded the sewage farm, and council nurseries were set up, together with two new cottages, so this one experienced a fragrant change of name.

156.   Here is one of the last hay harvests in Rayners Lane, *c.*1930, garnered from the fields as they receded before the houses whose advance can be seen through the trees.

157.   The first house built in the Pinner part of Rayners Lane contained one or two dwellings for the farm workers of Daniel Hill of Church Farm (*see* no.5). Dating from the 19th-century it was for decades the home of members of the Rayner family, from whom the lane ultimately derived its name. The building, seen from the north *c*.1910, stood on the site of the present nos.464-468.

158. Tom Rayner was born in the Rayners Lane cottage in 1852, the youngest child of George and Ann, but, orphaned in infancy, he grew up with his grandparents at the first *White Hart*, 26 High Street (*see* no.2). He became a stoker at the gas works and lived most of his adult life at Oak Cottages in Eastcote Road (*see* no.97). He was also a stalwart of the volunteer fire brigade.

159. This house with barns and haystack is hardly recognisable as no.552 Rayners Lane. It was a short-lived 20th-century farm, called Lankers Brook Farm, formed out of Church Farm after the death of Daniel Hill in 1906.

160.   Here is Rayners Lane in the late 1920s during its last days as a rural thoroughfare. It is taken from the slope up to the station, looking towards the farm cottages in the distance. The avenue of elms, still remembered by many, lasted until cut down by Dutch Elm disease in 1977.

161.   This is the same scene less than a decade later. By 1933 Village Way had been laid out, telegraph poles were ready for the forthcoming rush of subscribers, and shops were going up. The building housed the National Provincial Bank.

162.　North of Rayners Lane station the Metropolitan Country Estates Company developed Harrow Garden Village and advertised it in its Metroland booklets. The Close was laid out either side of the avenue of elms, well behind the shops in no.161, by E. S. Reid, the chief builder of the village. This is the first house, no.1, at its earliest stage in 1934, looking north. It was designed by Frank Field, whose designs were used by local building firms like Reid and Cutler.

163.　No.1 is near completion. At the side is the garden of the adjoining house, and at the rear are the first houses in Village Way.

164. No.1 is finished and occupied. On 3 November 1940 it was half shattered by an enemy bomb, and was rebuilt in a different style after the war.

165. Frank and Ivy Field, the delighted owners of no.1, who had photographed its progress. Mrs. Field and her children were inside the house when the bomb fell, and were very lucky to escape injury.

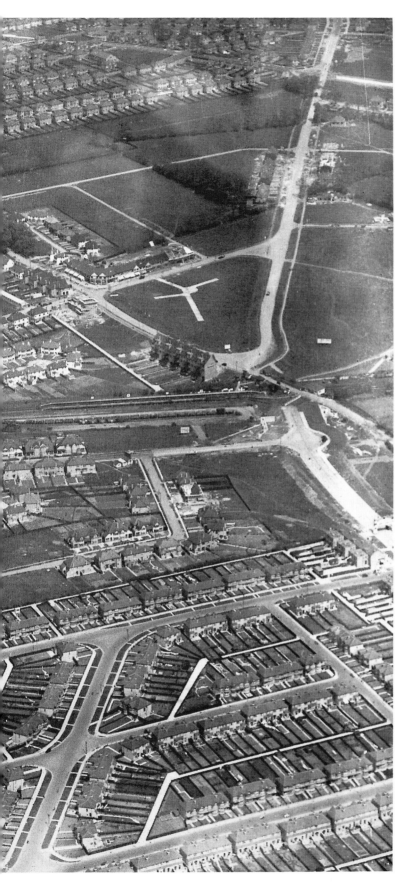

166. This is the Rayners Lane area of south Pinner in May 1934. By the station (centre right) Alexandra Avenue has yet to cross the railway and connect with Imperial Drive. Part of Harrow Garden Village is in place north of Village Way, which forms a triangle with Rayners Lane and Imperial Drive. The avenue of elms is clear, and no.1 stands out on its triangular site at the bottom corner of The Close. Just beyond the elms is the razed site of the Rayners' cottages, while at the top right a new parish hall and an empty plot await St Alban's Church. Nash's estate spreads south of the railway. The old field pattern shows through like a ghost.

167.   At Rayners Lane ticket office there was no shelter for the queue when this northward looking view was taken in September 1929. The white-gated entrance to the 'down' platform is at the left, while the way to the other is past the office. The clump of high trees at the right is the avenue of elms.

168.   Rayners Lane bridge was reconstructed in 1936. The lane runs across from top to bottom. In the left foreground the pedestrian is moving towards the unfinished Alexandra Avenue, and the shops with the round tower will arise where the placard advertises flats. A slightly realigned Imperial Drive will enter between Nash's estate hut and the further hut, which was Reid's. Beyond Reid's, the two shops in course of construction are nos.328 and 330 Rayners Lane, with the rear of Village Way behind to their right. The site of Nash's estate office is now part of the embankment, and the hut which had been Reid's coal office hung on for a good 50 years until it was burnt down in 1985.

169.   The imposing Pinner County School was built as a grammar school in Beaulieu Drive in 1937 and has reflected the changes in local education. Reorganisation converted it into a sixth form college in 1975, and a further restructuring resulted in the conveyance of the premises in 1982 to Heathfield, a private school for girls whose Harrow buildings were required for the St Ann's Centre.

170.　About a score of young men from Pinner served in the second Boer War, some with distinction, some at the cost of their lives. Many, maybe all, of them were given a public send-off and return welcome by the village worthies. This young man was Thomas Ellement, grandson of Thomas the builder (*see* no.85), who was with the Imperial Yeomanry, became a Rough Rider, and sergeant major, and was mentioned in dispatches. In later life he became a local councillor.

171.   It is a truism to say that the First World War had an impact on the people back at home greater than that of any previous war. The community strove in various ways to provide extra funds and comforts, as this poster for a garden party at Nower Hill House (*see* no.64) shows.

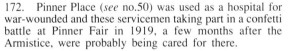

PINNER WAR WORKERS' GUILD.

A

GARDEN PARTY

In Aid of the Funds of the above,

WILL BE HELD AT

NOWER HILL,

(kindly lent by MRS. HEAL),

— ON —

Saturday, July 8th, 1916,

3 till 7.30 p.m.

A SHORT ADDRESS WILL BE GIVEN BY

Mrs. HAROLD MONTAGU

(Central Depot, Surgical Branch Queen Mary's Needlework Guild)

TENNIS, CROQUET, GAMES,

COMPETITIONS, Etc.   TEA 4.30.

Tickets (including Tea) - - 2s. 6d.

To be obtained of the Secretary of the Pinner Club, and Tradesmen.

GUILD.

ENTRANCE AFTER 6 P.M.   -   -   ONE SHILLING.

"Observer" Printing Works, Station Road, Harrow.

172.   Pinner Place (*see* no.50) was used as a hospital for war-wounded and these servicemen taking part in a confetti battle at Pinner Fair in 1919, a few months after the Armistice, were probably being cared for there.

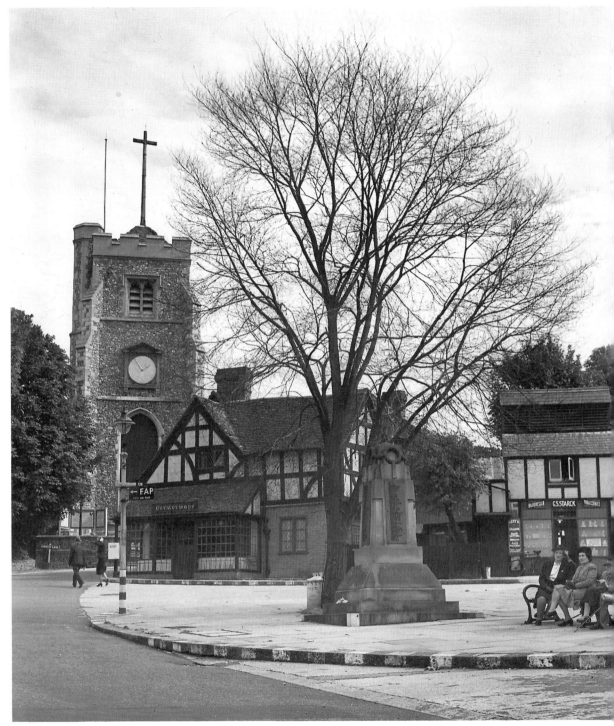

173. This picture unites the two world wars. It was taken in autumn 1944 and shows the First World War Memorial, to which many more names were so soon to be added, and several evidences of the current conflict. The kerbs, lamp-post, and even the plinth of the memorial, are marked with white paint so that they could be seen more easily during the blackout; the great west window of the church is boarded up against damage from air raids; there is a sign on the lamp-post pointing the way to the nearby First Aid Post; and the dustbin by the tree is for waste food not collected elsewhere, to be used as pigfood.

174.   England really was a home front during the war. The brick shelter outside the *Queen's Head* is typical of those put up in public places for general use—here, too, white warning paint is in use and the pub door is boarded up to shield the light during blackout.

175.   In Chapel Lane a British Restaurant was built where meals could be bought in the days of severe food rationing. The railway embankment can be seen behind it, but the hump in front is the roof of a long, semi-underground public shelter. Although it was a light structure, the restaurant building served many subsequent purposes and lasted until 1992. The one at North Harrow still stands in Station Road.

176.   A cartoon by Bert Thomas, a famous cartoonist of the time, who lived at Church Farm.

177.   Pinner did do its stuff. Many were the united efforts to raise extra funds for prisoners' parcels and for weapons. This is the float of the Colne Valley Electric Light Company chugging past Love Lane as part of the pageant for Warship Week 21-28 March 1942. The uniformed men are probably members of the Home Guard.

178.   The favourite pre-war holiday venue, the seaside, was almost wholly out of bounds in the south, so more effort was put into local alternatives. Harrow Council's Holidays at Home programme is staging a show at the rear of this fête at West End Recreation Ground in 1943.

179.   In 1945 came the peace, and here is a typical scene of rejoicing, a street party, which might have been followed by dancing in the evening. Some neighbourhoods managed one for each of the victories—in Europe and in Japan—but which this one celebrates is not known. It took place in The Close, off Pinner Hill Road, beside a substantial line of air raid shelters.

PINNER FAIR
1885.

180.   Pinner's ancient fair always takes place in the streets for just one day. It was purely a fun-fair by the time this photograph was taken in 1885. The Pettigrove family continues to bring its roundabouts to the same spot each year.

181. The Pettigrove horses are more clearly seen at the fair of 1914. So are the forces of law and order.

182. Off until next year! Rather more nostalgic than the later motorised transporters are the horse-drawn caravans and wagons shown in this High Street scene of packing up after the fair of c.1920.